PARENT-TEACHER COLLECTION

Write It Out

Mastering Short and Extended Responses to Open-Ended Questions: Level C

Coach™
America's Best for Student Success®

Triumph Learning®

A Haights Cross Communications ®️ Company

About the Authors

Sheila Crowell and *Ellen Kolba* are specialists in the teaching of writing and in preparing students for writing assessments. Their textbooks provide the affirmative support and scaffolding all students need to become better, more confident writers and to improve their scores on writing assessments.

As staff developers and writing curriculum specialists, Crowell and Kolba show teachers how to evaluate writing by first identifying and specifying the strengths in a draft, then making suggestions based on those strengths to prompt revision. To support the teaching of writing in their own school district in Montclair, New Jersey, they developed *The Writers' Room*™ Program, which trains volunteers from the community, pre-service teachers, and students to serve as writing coaches in elementary, middle, and high school Language Arts and English classes.

Under their direction, *The Writers' Room*™ Program has been brought to schools in Elizabeth, Metuchen, and Trenton, New Jersey, as well as to districts in New York, California, and Canada.

Acknowledgments

Special thanks to our writing team for their
help with this book:

Caleb E. Crowell

Marsha Kalman

Derek Kipp

Write It Out, Mastering Short and Extended Responses to Open-Ended Questions: Level C
125NA
ISBN-10: 1-59823-026-3
ISBN-13: 978-1-59823-026-0

Authors: Sheila Crowell and Ellen Kolba
Cover Image: Julie Delton/Photodisc/Green/Getty Images

Triumph Learning® 136 Madison Avenue, 7th Floor, New York, NY 10016
Kevin McAliley, President and Chief Executive Officer

10 9 8

Table of Contents

Part A: Writing Short Answers

Table of Contents

Part B: Writing Extended Answers

To the Student

In school, you have to take lots of tests.

Many test questions give you a choice of answers. You must pick the correct answer from the list of choices. Questions like these are called *multiple-choice questions*.

Another type of test question asks you to write something in your own words. Questions like these, which ask you to write your own answers instead of choosing from a multiple-choice list, are often called *open-ended questions*. They might also be called *constructed-response* or *extended-response questions*. This book is about these kinds of questions.

Open-ended questions are important! An open-ended question counts for more on a test than a multiple-choice question does. So it's important to learn how to write good answers to this kind of question.

Your score on an open-ended question depends on two things:

　　1) How well you understood the reading selection.

　　2) How well you expressed your answer in writing.

This book will give you practice in doing both.

An open-ended question may call for a short answer or a extended answer.

- A short-answer response contains only a few sentences or a paragraph.
- A extended-answer response may take two paragraphs or more—even a page.

In this book, you will practice writing both short and extended responses to open-ended questions. By the time you get to the end of the book, you should be ready to handle most open-ended questions on a real test.

So let's get started!

5 Rules for Writing Good Answers

Open-ended questions are based on a reading selection. When taking such a test, you first need to read the selection, then answer the questions that follow. So in order to practice writing open-ended questions, you need to start with a reading selection.

When you turn the page, you'll see a selection for you to read. Read it carefully. All the questions in the rest of this introduction are about this selection. You may read the selection as many times as you like if you need help to answer the questions.

This introduction will also show you five good rules for writing good answers. We call these rules the **SLAMS** rules. Look at the underlined letter in each rule. At the end of the introduction, you'll see why.

Now turn the page to begin reading about Betty, the Crow.

Betty the Crow

What is the smartest animal in the world? Is it a chimp? A dolphin? Your dog or cat?

Before you decide, meet Betty the Crow. Betty lives in a lab, where scientists study her and other crows. One day the scientists tried an experiment to see how smart crows are. They put Betty's favorite food in a small bucket. They lowered the bucket into a clear plastic tube. Betty could see the food, but she couldn't get to it.

The scientists gave Betty a hook made from a bent wire. They waited to see what she would do. As the scientists watched, another, bigger crow hopped over and stole Betty's hook!

That didn't stop Betty. She took a straight piece of wire. She tucked one end under the tape that held the plastic tube upright. Then, with her beak, she bent the wire into a hook. She lowered the hook into the tube and pulled up the bucket of food by its handle.

The scientists tested her over and over. Each time she used a different method to bend the wire.

The scientists were amazed. Betty was doing something that no bird or animal had ever done before. She was taking something never found in nature—a wire—and making a tool out of it.

Can other crows do what Betty did? What else can Betty do? The scientists are eager to find out, but one thing is clear. Betty is a lot smarter than anybody thought a bird could be.

Here is an open-ended question you might find on a test:

> **The selection tells about a smart crow named Betty. What did Betty do that shows she is smart?**

Ben's Answer:

made tools

Ben's answer is correct. Betty did make tools. But Ben's answer probably would not get a high score. Can you figure out why? It is not written in a complete sentence.

Ben's answer would have been better if he had written it like this:

Betty showed how smart she was when she made a tool.

Rule 1

Answers to open-ended questions should always be written in complete sentences. (Exception: When you fill out a chart.)

Here is another open-ended question:

> **Tell something that people can do that shows how smart they are.**

Minna's Answer:

talk

Rewrite Minna's answer so that it would get a better score.

_____

_____

_____

Rule 2: <u>L</u>ine Length=Answer Length

10

When writing the answer to an open-ended question, it's sometimes hard to know how long your answer should be. Here's a rule to help you know:

If your handwriting is big, you'll take about one-and-a-half lines to write a sentence. If you write small, you'll need only one line for a sentence.

> ## Rule 2
>
> The number of lines on the test gives you a good idea about how long your answer should be.

✓ So, if you see three or four lines, you probably should write at least three sentences.

✓ If you see a whole page of lines, you probably should write at least two paragraphs. If you see two whole pages of lines, then you should write at least three paragraphs, maybe more.

Denise read this question on a test:

How did Betty the Crow make a tool?

Denise's Answer:

She bent a wire.
_____

_____

_____

_____

Can you figure out what Denise did wrong? Denise's sentence is correct, but her answer is too short. To make it longer, she should add details from the selection.

On the lines after Denise's answer, write two more sentences that add details about how Betty the Crow, bent the wire. Remember to write in complete sentences.

This is not as easy as it looks! You have to be careful. You must understand the question, and you must answer all parts of the question. Also, you must give information that belongs with the answer.

Read this question:

> **The selection says that scientists gave Betty the Crow, a piece of wire bent into a hook. Why didn't she use it?**

Carlos's Answer:

Betty didn't use the hook that the scientists gave her. She made her own hook. She used the hook that she made herself.

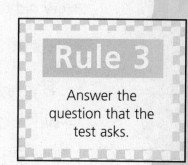

Rule 3

Answer the question that the test asks.

Shawana's Answer:

Betty didn't use the hook that the scientists gave her because a bigger crow hopped over and stole it.

The information in both answers is true, but Carlos's answer is not a good one. **He did not answer what the question asks.**

✓ The question doesn't ask *what* hook Betty used. It asks *why* she didn't use the hook the scientists gave her.

Shawana's answer is much better. She answers the question that was asked.

Try it. Answer this question using the information from the selection:

> **Why did the scientists use clear plastic for the tube?**

_____

_____

_____

Rule 4: **M**echanics Count

Rule 4

Mechanics are important. You should have no mistakes.

When writers—or teachers—talk about "mechanics," they don't mean people who fix things. In writing, mechanics means spelling, punctuation, and capitalization. Mechanics also means correct grammar and good word choices.

Suppose you write a good answer, but it has a few mistakes in spelling or punctuation. You will not get a low score. But suppose you make a lot of sloppy or careless mistakes. Then you will lose points.

Read the question, then read Marc's answer.

How did the scientist set up the experiement for Betty the Crow?

Marc's Answer:

The sientists put bettys food in a buket with a handel they put it in a clear plastic tube. So bety could see it. they put tap around the bottom of the tub so it would stand up strait. Then they gave her a wire hook

What do you notice? Marc's answer has a lot of supporting details, but it also has a lot of mistakes. It has:

✓ 7 spelling mistakes

✓ 1 run-on sentence and 1 incomplete sentence (a fragment)

✓ 5 mistakes in capitalization (1 because of the run-on sentence and 1 because of the fragment)

✓ 1 mistake with apostrophes (a missing apostrophe)

✓ 2 missing periods (1 because of the run-on sentence)

Marc did not pay attention to mechanics. His answer would not get a high score because of all the mistakes.

Rewrite Marc's answer with no mistakes on another sheet of paper.

This is probably the most important rule of all. Many students don't pay enough attention to it. If you forget everything else, remember this rule!

Support means to include information that explains or adds to your answer.

✓ For some questions, most of the support comes from the selection.

✓ For other questions, it is okay to add your own opinions, but you MUST include some information from the selection, no matter what you write.

Read the question and the answers that follow.

> **Why did the scientists put the food inside a tube, and why did they choose a tube made of clear plastic? Support your answer with details from the selection.**

Frida's Answer:

The scientists put the food in a tube. It was part of an experiment. It may seem strange to us, but scientists most of the time know what they are doing. But I don't think it's important to know how smart a crow is.

Antonia's Answer:

The scientists wanted to see how smart crows are. They put food at the bottom of a tube so Betty would have to use a hook to get it out. They used a clear plastic tube so Betty could see the food.

Rule 5

Support your answers with details from the selection.

Did Frida do a good job explaining?	___Yes ___ No
Did she explain why the tube was made of clear plastic?	___Yes ___ No
Did Antonia do a good job of explaining ?	___Yes ___ No
Did she explain why the tube was made of clear plastic?	___Yes ___ No

Below are details that Frida and Antonia wrote. Check which ones are from the selection and which ones are NOT from the selection.

Frida:

It was part of an experiment.

___from the selection   ___NOT from the selection

Scientists most of the time know what they are doing.

___from the selection   ___NOT from the selection

It's not important to know how smart a crow is.

___from the selection   ___NOT from the selection

Antonia:

The scientists wanted to see how smart crows are.

___from the selection   ___NOT from the selection

They put the food in a tube so Betty would have to use a hook to get it out.

___from the selection   ___NOT from the selection

They used a clear plastic tube so Betty could see the food.

___from the selection   ___NOT from the selection

Read and answer the following question. Be sure to look back at the selection for details that support your opinion.

> **The selection says, "Betty was doing something that no bird or animal had ever done before." What was it? Support your answer with details from the selection.**

_____

_____

_____

_____

_____

SLAMS—A Memory Gem

To help you remember the five rules in this chapter, remember this word: SLAMS!

 stands for **S**entence. Write your answers in complete sentences.

 stands for **L**ines. The number of lines on the answer sheet gives you an idea of how long your answer should be.

stands for **A**nswer. Answer the question that the test asks. Answer all parts of the question. Read the question a few times to make sure you understand what the question asks.

 stands for **M**echanics. Mechanics are punctuation, capitalization, spelling, grammar, and usage. Your sentence mechanics should be correct. You should write without mistakes.

stands for **S**upport. Remember to support your answer with details from the selection.

When you answer open-ended questions, try to recall this memory gem. Give your answers the *SLAMS* test. If your answer doesn't follow all of the *SLAMS* rules, fix it!

Remember—a good answer **SLAMS** the question!

Scoring Rubric

Every test has a different way of scoring the answers to an open-ended question. One of the most common methods is a scale of 0 to 4. The highest score is a 4; the lowest score is 0.

It might help if you know what you need to get a 4 or a 3. Here are some rubric guidelines for answering open-ended questions.

SCORE   **WHAT IT MEANS**

You answered the question clearly and completely.

You included ideas from the reading selection that are on target.

You supported these ideas with details and examples.

If the question asked you to, you connected the ideas from the reading selection to your own ideas and experiences.

You answered in complete and interesting sentences.

SCORE   **WHAT IT MEANS**

You answered the question.

You included some ideas from the reading selection.

You used some examples and details for support.

If the question asked you to, you connected some of the ideas from the reading selection to your own experiences.

Most of your sentences were complete.

SCORE   **WHAT IT MEANS**

You only answered part of the question.

You only included one or two ideas or details from the reading selection. The main ideas may not have been included.

You didn't connect your own ideas or experiences with the reading passage.

Many of your sentences were written incorrectly.

SCORE   **WHAT IT MEANS**

You didn't seem to understand the reading selection.

Your answer didn't include the important details from the selection.

You didn't connect your ideas to the reading passage.

You often wrote only single words or groups of words instead of complete sentences.

SCORE   **WHAT IT MEANS**

You didn't write anything; OR

You didn't answer the question asked.

Unit 1

Main Idea

Everything you read has a ***main idea***. A main idea is a big idea. Another word for main idea is ***topic***. The main idea is what the whole reading selection is about.

Whenever you read, you should look for the main idea. Think about the main idea of each paragraph. Then think about how these ideas are connected. This will help you figure out the one big idea—the main idea—of the whole selection.

Knowing the main idea makes it easier to understand what the author wants you to know.

In this unit, you will learn more about how to identify the main idea.

Lesson 1

What Makes a Good Answer?

Read the selection *Welcome to the Community* before answering the question on the next page.

Welcome to the Community

Look for an important word that tells you what this passage is mostly about.

Maybe you live on a farm in the country. Maybe you live in an apartment in the city. Maybe you live in a house in the suburbs. No matter where you live, you're part of a community. A city is a large community. People who live on the same block make up a smaller community. The smallest community of all is your family.

People who live in a small community, like a family, take care of one another. Think about your family. In a family, a few people work together to do many jobs—make meals, clean the home, take care of children, and shop for food and clothes. Adults, like parents and caretakers, do a lot of the work, but children often help, too.

A larger community, like a city, has even more work to do. To get everything done, different people do different jobs. Some community workers keep you safe. Some help you get better when you are sick. Other people keep the city clean, drive you from place to place, or deliver your mail. Still others teach you how to become a good member of the community when you are older.

The main idea is repeated in the last sentence.

Whether a community is small or large, people have to work together to make it a good place to live.

Now read this question. Base your answer on *Welcome to the Community*.

What is the main idea of this selection? Support your answer with details from the selection.

Mary Beth's Answer:

Mary Beth wrote a good answer to this question. Read her answer below.

The main idea of this selection is that people who live in a community have to work together. Parents do most of the work in a family. They cook and clean and shop. Kids help, too. A city is a larger community. People do many different jobs. They all work together to make the city a good place to live.

What Makes Mary Beth's Answer Work?

Mary Beth does what the test scorers are looking for.

✓ She repeats part of the question in her opening sentence. This focuses her answer.

✓ She chooses important details from the selection to support her answer.

✓ She writes interesting and complete sentences.

HINT!

The people who score the test look for the following things:

✳ A clear and complete sentence that tells the main idea.

✳ Details from the selection that support your first sentence.

✳ Complete, correct, and interesting sentences.

1. Mary Beth's answer starts with a topic sentence. This sentence repeats part of the question, and then it states the main idea.

   What is Mary Beth's topic sentence? Write it here.

   _____

   _____

   _____

2. In her answer, Mary Beth uses details from the selection to support her topic sentence. One detail is that adults do most of the work in a family.

   Find another sentence with a supporting detail. Write it here.

   _____

   _____

   _____

3. Mary Beth first discusses the family, which is a small community. Then she compares the family to a larger community.

   How does Mary Beth compare these two communities in her answer? Write the sentences that describe the larger community here.

   _____

   _____

   _____

4. Mary Beth ends her answer with an interesting concluding sentence. This sentence sums up the main idea.

   What is Mary Beth's conclusion? Write her sentence here.

   _____

   _____

   _____

Tools & Tips

How to Find the Main Idea
of a Paragraph

Step 1: Find the **topic sentence**. The topic sentence states the main idea of a paragraph. It tells what the paragraph is about. In many paragraphs, the topic sentence is the first sentence. It also can be the last sentence.

Step 2: Sometimes a paragraph does not have a topic sentence. Then you have to figure out the main idea.
Here's how:

- ✓ Read the whole paragraph.
- ✓ Pay attention to all the details.
- ✓ Use the details to figure out the main idea.

Find the main idea in the following paragraph.

> At one table, kids work on a school project. In a chair in the corner, a man reads a magazine. A woman types a letter in the computer room. People line up at the desk to check out books. Children sit on the rug, listening to a story.

What is the main idea of this paragraph? Put an X next to the correct answer.

_____ **A.** People of all ages are busy.

_____ **B.** A library is filled with books.

_____ **C.** People visit the library for many reasons.

_____ **D.** You have to be able to read to get a library card.

Lesson 2

Revising and Improving a Weak Answer

Here is another reading selection. To answer the question that follows, you must find supporting details that tell about the main idea.

A Visit to City Hall

The main idea is expressed in this paragraph.

Where do you sign up for a town sports team? Where do adults register to vote? Where can you attend a town meeting and speak up about community issues that matter to you? You can do all these things at City Hall. Many people who help run your community work here.

One of these people is the mayor. The mayor is in charge of the town. Being mayor is a big job. The mayor must fill job, like the police chief and the fire chief. The mayor also leads town council meetings and signs new laws. On special days, the mayor marches in parades and makes speeches.

This paragraph is loaded with supporting details.

The mayor gets a lot of help from the other people who work at City Hall. The town clerk registers people to vote. The clerk also keeps track of birth certificates and other important records. The office of public works deals with recycling and trash collection. The transportation office takes care of traffic lights, parking meters, and road repairs. The recreation office is in charge of parks, swimming pools, and sports leagues.

Running a town is too big a job for just one person. All the people at City Hall work together to make a town run smoothly.

Read this question.

> **What is this selection mainly about? Support your answer with details from the selection.**

Oliver's Answer:

Oliver wrote an answer to this question, but it is not very good.

> I signed up for soccer. There was a long line.

Improving Oliver's Answer

Oliver's answer would not get a good score because it does not answer the question. He does not tell what the selection is mainly about. He does not include any details from the selection. His answer should be longer, too.

How could Oliver improve his answer? Use the questions below and on the next page to help improve Oliver's answer.

1. Oliver needs to pay attention to the question. He needs to tell what the selection is mainly about.

   Look at the question again. What is the main idea of the selection? Write a new opening sentence for Oliver.

   _____

   _____

   _____

   _____

HINT!

The people who score the test look for the following things:

* A clear and complete sentence that tells the main idea.

* Details from the selection that **support** the answer, or **supporting details**.

* Complete, correct, and interesting sentences.

2. Oliver does not use any details from the selection to support his answer. One detail that he could use is that running a town is too big a job for just one person.

Check the reading selection for more details. Write two new sentences of your own that give examples that support your opening sentence.

_____

_____

_____

_____

3. **Now rewrite Oliver's answer here.**

_____

_____

_____

_____

_____

_____

_____

_____

_____

_____

HINT!

Make sure the answer meets all the **SLAMS** tests.

SCORE BUILDER

Before you forget—

What is the memory gem word?

_____

What does each letter stand for?

1 _____

_____

2 _____

_____

3 _____

_____

4 _____

_____

5 _____

_____

Lesson 3

Responding on Your Own

In this selection, you will read about another community helper. The question that follows asks you to think of a title for the selection and explain why you chose that title. Don't forget what you have learned from studying Mary Beth's and Oliver's answers.

Look for the main idea in this paragraph.

If your teacher asked you to make a list of community helpers, who would be on it? Most lists would include police officers and firefighters. Doctors and teachers would be on the list, too. Would garbage collectors be on your list? They should be!

What supporting detail can you find in this paragraph?

Think about what your town would be like without garbage collectors. Trash piles would get bigger and bigger. Soon trash would be everywhere. Your town would be a big, dirty mess. People would get sick, too. Garbage is a good place for germs to grow.

Collecting garbage is not easy. All day long, garbage collectors pick up heavy trashcans and empty them into trucks. Every day, each worker picks up about 15 tons of trash. That's like picking up three or four elephants!

Garbage collectors work in all kinds of weather. In the heat of the summer, they handle trash that smells terrible. In the cold of the winter, they put plows on their trucks and clear the snowy streets.

People don't think much about their trash. They don't think about the men and women who take it away, either. If they did, they would realize that garbage collectors have one of the most important jobs in the community.

Read this question.

Choose a title for this selection. Use information from the selection to explain why your title is a good one. Write your answer on the lines below.

My Title

_____

_____

Why I Chose It

_____

_____

_____

_____

_____

_____

_____

_____

_____

_____

_____

_____

_____

_____

HINT!

When you are finished, check your answer:

* Does your title tell what the selection is mainly about?

* What details from the selection support your title?

* Does your explanation meet all the SLAMS tests?

Reader's Response!
Revise & Edit

When you have finished writing about the selection, exchange papers with a partner. As you read each other's work, answer the questions below.

1 Did the writer fully answer BOTH parts of the question? ___Yes ___ No
If not, what needs to be added or changed?
Write your response on the lines below.

_____

_____

2 Do you think the writer chose a good title? ___ Yes ___ No
If you do, explain why. If you don't, explain why not.
Write your response on the lines below.

_____

_____

3 Did the writer give clear reasons for his or her choice? ___ Yes ___ No
If not, what needs to be added or changed?
Write your response on the lines below.

_____

_____

4 Has the writer followed all the SLAMS rules? ___ Yes ___ No
If not, which rules were not followed?
Check all the rules that apply.

S ___   L ___   A ___   M ___   S ___

5 **Give the paper back to your partner to revise and edit.**

Reviewing the Question

When you are answering open-ended questions, it is important to be a careful reader. A question that asks you to find the main idea of a reading selection may not use the words **main idea** at all. Instead, you may see questions like these:

- What is this selection mainly about?

- In your own words, tell what this selection is about.

- What do you think would be a good title for this selection? Explain why the title you chose is a good one.

All of these questions are different ways of asking you to find the main idea of the reading selection. If you see a question like the ones above on a test, the question is asking you to explain the main idea.

Cause and Effect

If you tickle a baby's toes, the baby will start to laugh. This is an example of **cause and effect**.

You tickle the baby's toes. That is the **cause.**

The baby laughs. That is the **effect.**

Here is another example of cause and effect. One day as you walk to school, you trip on a curb. You drop your schoolbooks.

You trip on the sidewalk. That is the **cause**.

You drop your schoolbooks. That is the **effect**.

An open-ended question about **cause** wants you to explain **what makes something happen**.

An open-ended question about **effect** wants you to explain **why something happened**.

A question may ask you to describe **something that might happen,** even though it has yet to happen. For example, you may have to describe **what the result might be** if a character acts in a certain way. This is called **making a prediction**. Be sure that your predictions make sense. Your predictions should be based on what you learn as you read.

Lesson 4

What Makes a Good Answer?

Read this selection. The question that follows asks you to think about cause and effect. Use details from the selection to support your answer.

Big Questions

Why is the sky blue? How do fish breathe underwater? Why do leaves change color in the fall? Where does the sun go at night? These are questions that a lot of kids wonder about.

Scientists wonder about these things, too. Scientists want to explain the world around them. They want to find out how things work. So do kids. You could say that kids are natural-born scientists!

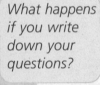

What happens if you write down your questions?

What questions do you have? When you think of a question, you can write it down in a special notebook. This notebook will be your science journal. Writing down your questions will help you remember them.

When you have time, try to find the answers to your questions. You can ask a grown-up. You might want to go to the library or use the computer to look for answers. Then write the answers in your journal.

Don't be surprised if you start to think of more and more questions. You may find that the more you learn, the more you will want to know!

Read this question.

> **Why should you write down your questions in a science journal? Support your answer with details from the selection.**

Jorge's Answer:

Jorge wrote a good answer to this question.

If you write down your questions in a science journal, then you won't forget them. You should write the answers in your notebook, too. Scientists ask lots of questions. Asking questions is a good way to learn new things. Soon you will be thinking like a scientist. The more you ask, the more you learn!

What Makes Jorge's Answer Work?

Let's look more closely at how Jorge answered the question.

1. Jorge starts out with a sentence that shows both cause and effect. Notice that this sentence states his main idea.

   What is Jorge's main idea sentence? Write it here. Draw a line under the part of the sentence that shows *cause*. Circle the part of the sentence that shows *effect*.

   _____

   _____

   _____

2. In his answer, Jorge uses details from the selection to support his topic sentence.

   Find one sentence with a supporting detail. Write it here.

   _____

   _____

   _____

3. In his answer, Jorge writes: Asking questions is a good way to learn *new things*.

   If *asking questions* is the cause, what is the effect? Write the effect part of the sentence here.

   _____

   _____

4. Jorge gives his answer an interesting conclusion.

   What is Jorge's concluding sentence? Write it here.

   _____

   _____

   _____

Tools & Tips

Questions that ask you to explain cause and effect can be written in different ways. You might not always see the exact words, *cause* or *effect*, in the question. If you read carefully, you will find some clues.

Here are some clues that help you know when a question is asking you to explain the **cause**:

Why…?

What is the reason for…?

What do you think would happen if…?

Here are some clues that help you know when a question is asking you to explain the **effect**:

as a result	**because**	**so**	**for**
since	**so that**	**therefore**	**then**

Read this question. What clue do you see? Is the clue about *cause* or *effect*?

Why do scientists do experiments?

Write the your answers here.

_____

_____

Look for these clues when you read. Pay attention to them. They can help you answer questions about the selection.

Lesson 5

Revising and Improving a Weak Answer

Here is another reading selection. To answer the question that follows, you must find supporting details.

Floppy Bones

Why are we able to stand up straight? Our bones are strong! Our bones support our muscles. Without bones, we could not walk or run. Bones also protect our hearts and lungs and other organs. It is important to make sure that our bones stay strong and healthy.

Doctors tell us that calcium helps build strong bones. Calcium is a mineral. It is found in different foods. Milk and cheese have a lot of calcium. So do broccoli and other green leafy vegetables. You can even buy special orange juice with extra calcium in it.

What supporting details about calcium can you find in this paragraph?

If you want to see what happens to bones that do not get enough calcium, try this experiment. Put a clean chicken bone in a bowl. Pour vinegar into the bowl until the bone is covered with vinegar. Check the bone every day. Keep checking it for a week.

At the end of the week, take the bone out of the vinegar. Look at it. You will see that the bone has gotten smaller. Touch the bone. It will feel soft and rubbery.

This paragraph shows a cause-and-effect relationship.

What happened? The acid in the vinegar took out the calcium in the bone. The bone became weak when it lost its calcium. If we don't get enough calcium in our diets, our bones will get weak, too.

Read this question.

Why is calcium important for our bones? Support your answer with details from the selection.

Arden's Answer:

Arden wrote an answer to this question, but the answer is not very good.

> I drink lots of milk. Cookies taste good with milk. Another drink I like is soda.

Improving Arden's Answer

Arden's answer would not get a good score because it does not answer the question.

✓ Arden did not explain why strong bones are important. Instead, Arden writes that she drinks lots of milk. Then she mentions cookies and soda.

✓ Arden needs to begin with a sentence that starts to answer the question. She needs to include details from the selection, too. Her answer also needs to be a bit longer. How could Arden improve her answer?

HINT!

The people who score the test look for the following things:

* A clear and complete statement of cause and effect.

* Details from the selection that support the answer.

* Complete, correct, and interesting sentences.

1. Arden needs to pay more attention to the question.

    Read the question again. Write a new opening sentence, or topic sentence, for Arden.

    _____

    _____

    _____

2. Arden does not use many details from the selection to support her answer.

Find more details in *Floppy Bones* that support your topic sentence. Write two new sentences for Arden.

_____

_____

_____

3. Arden says that she drinks lots of milk, but she does not explain how milk helps to make her bones strong and healthy.

Find the missing information in *Floppy Bones*. Write two new sentences about the connection between drinking milk and having strong bones.

_____

_____

_____

4. **Combine all your sentences into one answer.**

_____

_____

_____

_____

_____

_____

_____

_____

HINT!

Make sure your
answer meets all the
SLAMS tests.

_____

_____

SCORE BUILDER

Test questions can be hard to figure out. Reading selections can have so much information! How do you know where to begin?

One way to start is to use the words from the question in your topic sentence. Then add a word like *because* or *so*, and complete your answer. Complete your answer with a detail from the selection. You will be off to a great start!

Here is an example.

Why did the bone get soft after sitting in vinegar?

You can write a topic sentence in several ways:

The bone got soft after sitting in vinegar because it lost its calcium.

Or:

The bone got soft after sitting in vinegar because the acid in the vinegar took the calcium away.

Try it! Read this question.

Why are foods like cheese and broccoli good for us?

Write a good beginning sentence here.

_____

_____

_____

Responding on Your Own

In this selection, you will read about a science experiment. The question that follows asks you to think about what you have read. Make sure to use information from the selection in your answer.

Hidden Rainbows

Write your name on a piece of paper with a black marker. Look closely at your writing. Did you know that a rainbow of colors is hiding inside the black letters?

Here is a way to see that rainbow. You will need a black water-based marker. You also will need a white paper coffee filter, a pair of scissors, a small plate, and a glass of water.

Cut out a circle from the paper coffee filter. The circle should be a little bit smaller than the plate. With the marker, draw a dot in the center of the paper circle. The dot should be about the size of a quarter. Put the paper on the plate. Then sprinkle a few drops of water onto the black dot. Wait a few minutes. Soon rings of different colors will start to move across the paper.

What causes the black color to turn into a rainbow?

You see different colors because the ink is not really black. It is a mixture of colors. When you write your name, the letters look black. The colors stay mixed together. But when you put water on the black ink, the colors start to move around. The coffee-filter paper absorbs the water and helps the colors spread out. You can see the rainbow of colors hidden inside the color black.

The experiment is the cause.

Read this question.

In *Hidden Rainbows*, you learned that black is made up of many colors. Why can't you see the colors? Use information from the selection to explain your answer.

Write your answer on the lines below.

_____

_____

_____

_____

_____

_____

_____

_____

_____

_____

_____

_____

_____

_____

_____

_____

_____

_____

_____

_____

HINT!

When you finish, check your answer.

* Does your answer use words that show cause and effect?

* Have you used details from the selection to explain your answer?

* Does your answer meet the SLAMS test?

Reader's Response!
Revise & Edit

When you have finished writing about *Hidden Rainbows*, exchange papers with a partner. As you read each other's work, answer the questions below.

1 Did the writer fully answer the question?　　　___Yes ___ No
If not, what needs to be added or changed?

Write your response here.

_____

_____

2 Did the writer use details from the selection and from personal knowledge to support his or her answer?　___ Yes ___ No
If not, what needs to be added or changed?

Write your response here.

_____

_____

_____

3 Was the answer clear and easy to understand?　___ Yes ___ No
If not, what needs to be added or changed?

Write your response here.

_____

_____

_____

4 Has the writer followed all the SLAMS rules?　___ Yes ___ No
If not, which rules were not followed?
Check all the rules that apply.

S ___　　L ___　　A ___　　M ___　　S ___

5 **Give the paper back to your partner to revise and edit.**

Reviewing the Question

Make sure you know the difference between *cause* and *effect*:

- Something that makes something else happen is the **cause**.

- The result, or the thing that happens, is the **effect**.

You will find cause-and-effect questions with all kinds of reading selections. **Informational selections** explain things. The questions will ask you to explain things, too.

- Why did something happen? **(cause)**

- What happened? **(effect)**

Stories usually tell about made-up characters and events. The questions will ask if you understand the story.

- Why did a character act a certain way? **(cause)**

- What event happened as a result of a character's actions? **(effect)**

Understanding Characters

The people or animals in a story are called the **characters**. When you read a story, you read about what the characters do and say. The characters' actions and words tell the story.

To understand a story, you need to understand the characters. The writer might not always explain *why* a character does the things he or she does. It is up to the reader to figure out what *motivates* the characters.

Don't worry! You don't have to figure it out by yourself. The writer gives clues that help you understand the characters. For example, the writer might tell you that a character is grinning, jumping up and down, and shouting "Yay! Hooray!" The writer might not tell you that the character is excited, but these words and actions show that the character is excited.

When you read a story, look for the writer's clues. Use your own experiences, too. Think about the people you know, and the ways they act. How can you tell when someone is happy or mad or shy? What do they do and say?

Lesson 7

What Makes a Good Answer?

Here is a short story, or *narrative*. It is the beginning of the story. Notice that the question, which follows the selection, asks you to figure out how the character feels.

Lilah Meets Gray Cat

Look for a clue word that tells you how Lilah feels about the purring sound.

Lilah heard the purring when she opened the back door, but she couldn't see the cat. Smiling, she tiptoed down the back steps and softly called, "Here, kitty."

The purring grew louder.

"Where are you?" Lilah asked. Then she saw the lower leaves of a bush move a little. Crouching down, she leaned forward and very slowly peered under the bush.

"Ooh," she said in a whisper. "There you are. Aren't you beautiful!"

The cat was a soft gray and very fluffy. Its green eyes blinked in the sun as it looked at Lilah. Slowly and lazily, the cat stretched out one paw and then the other. It purred more loudly, then rolled onto its back. With one paw, it reached for Lilah.

Lilah's actions tell you how she feels about the cat.

Lilah's smile grew and she reached out a finger to gently touch the cat's paw.

"I think maybe you need a home," Lilah said, "and a name. I'm going to call you Gray Cat."

Read the question.

Is Lilah happy to find the cat? How do you know? Use details from the story to support your answer.

Jeremy's Answer:

Jeremy's answer includes everything the test scorers look for. Read what Jeremy wrote. Then answer the questions that follow. The questions will help you understand what makes Jeremy's answer a good one.

> Lilah is happy to find the cat. You know because she is smiling. Also, she walks and talks very quietly so she won't scare the cat. She says the cat is beautiful, too. She gently touches the cat, then she says she wants to give the cat a home and a name.

HINT!

Remember that the test scorers will look for the following things:

* A clear statement of the main idea.

* Details from the selection that support the maiin idea.

* Complete, correct, and interesting sentences.

What Makes Jeremy's Answer Work?

Jeremy has understood both parts of the question. He then found the information to answer the question in the story. Here's how he did it:

✓ He read the story very carefully.

✓ He reread the question to make sure he understood it.

✓ He looked for details, or clues, in the story that tell how Lilah feels. These clues are the things Lilah says and does.

✓ Jeremy's details support his answer that Lilah is happy to find the cat.

Finally, Jeremy puts the details in an order that makes sense. When he writes his answer, he writes clear, complete sentences.

Now let's take a closer look at Jeremy's answer.

1. Jeremy states his main idea in the first sentence.

   What is the main idea? Write Jeremy's topic sentence here.

   _____

   _____

   _____

2. Jeremy includes details from the selection that support the main idea, or topic sentence. One detail is that Lilah is smiling.

   Find another supporting detail in Jeremy's answer. Write the sentence with that supporting detail here.

   _____

   _____

   _____

3. Jeremy puts the details in an order that makes sense. He uses words like *also* and *too* to help the reader follow the order.

   Find a sentence with a word that shows the order of ideas. Write that sentence here.

   _____

   _____

   _____

Tools & Tips

Remember that you need to support your answer with details from the story. You need to explain what the character says or does to show how the character feels.

Read these sentences. Look for clues that tell how the characters feel.

✓ Lilah **smiled** as the cat curled up in her lap and purred loudly.

✓ The cat jumped up to chase a leaf around the yard.

✓ Lilah's smile faded as the cat ran off.

Which sentence has clues that show that the cat is playful and full of energy? Write the clues in your own words.

_____

_____

_____

Which clues show that Lilah's feelings change? Write the clues in your own words.

_____

_____

_____

Revising and Improving a Weak Answer

Here is more of the story about Lilah and Gray Cat. The question on the next page asks you to explain something about a character in the story.

Gray Cat Has an Adventure

"Wait right here," Lilah said to Gray Cat. She ran into the house to get a dish of milk. When she came back, Gray Cat was gone. She looked all over the yard, calling for him.

"Here, kitty! Here, Gray Cat!"

Gray Cat was busy with a project of his own. An interesting smell had caught his attention. He followed it, his nose twitching and his tail swishing back and forth.

What do Gray Cat's actions tell you about him?

"Fish?" he wondered, "or maybe fish and cheese?"

Gray Cat followed the smells, walking onto a big, wide porch. Looking up, he saw a cage hanging above him. Inside sat a yellow bird. The bird began to sing.

Gray Cat plopped down and stared. The bird's singing grew louder and more excited, and the bird began to flap its wings.

"Now, that's interesting," thought Gray Cat.

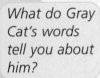
What do Gray Cat's words tell you about him?

Just then a woman came out of the house with a broom in her hand. "Go away!" she yelled at Gray Cat. She swatted at Gray Cat, and Gray Cat scurried down the stairs and dashed across the yard.

Read the question.

> **What is Gray Cat like? Use details from the story to support your answer.**

Angela's Answer:

Angela wrote an answer to this question, but it needs to be better.

The cat likes to walk around. Sniffing things. He watches a bird in a cage.

Improving Angela's Answer

Angela didn't do everything she should have to write a good answer. She does mention three things that the cat does, but her sentences are missing some things.

✓ She hasn't written a topic sentence—a sentence that states the main idea.

✓ Some sentences are incomplete sentences.

✓ The order of details does not make sense to the reader.

✓ Her answer is too short.

How could Angela improve her answer? Use the questions below and on page 52 to help you revise and improve Angela's answer.

1. Angela needs to state the main idea in a topic sentence.

   Read the question again. Write a topic sentence for Angela here.

   _____

   _____

   _____

HINT!

Remember to do the following when you write your answer:

* State your main idea clearly and completely in the first sentence.

* Use details from the selection to support your main idea.

* Write sentences that are complete, correct, and interesting.

2. Angela says that the cat likes to walk around and sniff things, but she doesn't say where he walked or why he walked. She also has an incomplete sentence.

   Check the reading selection for details. What details could you add that would support your topic sentence? Write two new sentences of your own here. Make sure your sentences are complete.

   _____

   _____

   _____

   _____

3. Angela says that the cat watched a bird in a cage. What does this detail tell us about Gray Cat?

   Write two sentences. In the first sentence, tell about Gray Cat and the bird. In the second sentence, tell what we learn about Gray Cat from this detail.

   _____

   _____

   _____

   _____

4. **Combine all your sentences into one answer.**

   _____

   _____

   _____

   _____

   _____

   _____

HINT!

Make sure your answer meets all the SLAMS tests.

SCORE BUILDER

Do you remember the first SLAMS rule? The first rule is: **_Write complete sentences._**

Every sentence in your answer needs to start with a capital letter:

Write complete sentences.

Every sentence needs to end with a period:

Write complete sentences.

Of course, if you write a question, you need to use a question mark at the end:

Did you write a complete sentence?

Here is one example of a complete sentence that Angela wrote in her answer.

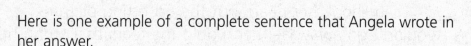
The cat likes to walk around.

Find another complete sentence in Angela's answer. Write it on the lines below.

_____

_____

_____

_____

Lesson 9

Responding on Your Own

Here is the rest of the story about Lilah and Gray Cat. The question on the next page asks you to explain how Lilah's feelings change during this part of the story. This time you will write the answer on your own. Use what you have learned from studying Jeremy's good answer and improving Angela's weak answer to help you write your own answer.

Gray Cat Returns

Lilah was sure she would never see Gray Cat again. She had looked all over the yard. She had put the dish of milk on the grass, hoping he would smell it. But there was no sign of him.

Lilah sat down on the back steps. Her heart felt heavy, and she thought of all the terrible things that might have happened to Gray Cat. Gray Cat might have gotten lost and not known his way back. He might have gotten into a fight with a dog, or he might have wandered onto a busy street, full of speeding cars.

Look for clues that tell you how Lilah feels.

Lilah shook her head, but the upsetting pictures wouldn't go away. Neither would the tears that stung her eyes and nose. She hadn't known Gray Cat very long, but she felt like Gray Cat had been hers forever.

And then she heard it, loud and clear—a purring sound.

"Gray Cat!" Lilah shouted with a grin.

Look for clues that tell you how Lilah feels now.

She flew down the stairs to meet him, her frown replaced by a broad smile. She laughed as she picked up the fluffy gray cat and hugged him to her.

Read this question. Write your answer on the lines below.

How does Lilah feel at the beginning of *Gray Cat Returns*? How does she feel at the end? Use details from the story to support your answer.

_____

_____

_____

_____

_____

_____

_____

_____

_____

_____

_____

_____

_____

_____

_____

_____

_____

_____

_____

HINT!

When you finish, check your answer.

* Have you stated the main idea clearly in the first sentence?

* Have you answered both parts of the question?

* Have you used details from the story to support your answer?

* Does your answer meet the SLAMS test?

Reader's Response!
Revise & Edit

When you have finished writing about *Gray Cat Returns*, exchange papers with a partner. As you read each other's work, answer the questions below.

1 Did the writer fully answer BOTH parts of the question?   ___ Yes ___ No

2 Do you think the writer's main idea is stated
clearly in the first sentence?   ___ Yes ___ No
If you do, explain why. If you don't, explain why not.

Write your response here.

_____

_____

_____

3 Did the writer use supporting details
from the selection?   ___ Yes ___ No
If not, what needs to be added or changed?

Write your response here.

_____

_____

_____

4 Has the writer followed all the SLAMS rules?   ___ Yes ___ No

If not, which rules were not followed?

Check the appropriate boxes.

S ___   L ___   A ___   M ___   S ___

5 **Give the paper back to your partner to revise and edit.**

Reviewing the Question

There is more than one way to ask a question about the characters in a story. Here are some questions about characters to help you. Pay attention to the words in **dark** type.

- What is a character **like**?

- How would you **describe** a character?

- How does a character **feel**?

- How are two characters **alike**?

- How are two characters **different**?

- How does a character **change**?

All these questions ask you to do the same thing—to tell about a character. To answer these questions, you need to figure out what kind of person or animal the character is. For example, is the character happy? Boring? Sad? Adventurous? Angry? Hard-working? Helpful? Lazy? Mean? Fun? What clues show you and tell you about the character?

Read the selection and answer the questions that follow.

The Story About the Bears

Let's get this straight. In that story about Goldilocks and the three bears, Goldilocks didn't have yellow hair. How do I know? I'm Papa Bear, and this isn't really the little girl's story. It's ours.

We live in a house in the woods—me, Mama, and Baby Bear. People don't understand us. They think we mean to hurt them when we only want to be left alone. One morning, we went out for a walk. It was such a beautiful day.

"Let's leave our cereal on the table," Mama suggested. "This sunshine is too good to waste."

It was the kind of walk we like best. We didn't see a soul. Finally, we headed home. "I can hardly wait to eat," said Baby Bear. Mama and I agreed. Those bowls of cereal we had left behind were looking better and better.

What did we find? Someone had been tasting our food, and Baby's bowl was completely empty! "Oh, no!" cried Baby.

That was just the start. The chairs were knocked over, and Baby's chair was broken to bits.

"Why does everything happen to me?" complained Baby. "I'm going back to bed." He stomped up the stairs.

At the top, he let out a terrified yell. "Help! Someone's broken into our house!"

Mama and I raced up the stairs. The covers on all three beds had been pulled back, and in Baby's bed lay a dark-haired girl. She sat up and rubbed her eyes. It looked like she'd been sleeping. She took a good look at us, screamed, and dashed out of the house.

Our jaws dropped with surprise. What was she so afraid of?

1 Main Idea

This story could have many different titles. Think of another title that would tell readers what the story is about. Write your new title on the lines below. Then explain why you chose it.

_____

_____

_____

_____

_____

_____

_____

_____

2 Cause and Effect

Why was Baby Bear so upset? Use details from the selection in your answer.

_____

_____

_____

_____

_____

_____

_____

_____

_____

3 Understanding Characters

How do you think the three bears felt about Goldilocks? Use details from the selection to support your answer.

_____

_____

_____

_____

_____

_____

_____

_____

_____

Unit 4

Reading What Is on the Page

Your first job as a reader is to **read what is on the page**. That means finding and understanding information in the text.

When you read what is on the page, you look for two things:

- the main idea
- the details that support the main idea

A question about what is on the page asks for information that is in the selection. It *doesn't* ask you to figure out anything that is *not* in the selection.

- It might ask you to **retell** part of a story in your own words.

- It might ask you to **describe** a process in your own words.

Lesson 10

What Makes a Good Answer?

Let's read about a way to make good, fresh soil for a garden. After you read, answer the questions that test how well you can describe this process.

The Secret to the Garden

Amy thought her Aunt Lea's garden had the tallest, strongest plants she had ever seen. One night, after dinner at her aunt's house, Amy asked, "Aunt Lea, why is your garden so amazing?"

"Help me with the dishes first," said Aunt Lea. "Then I'll show you."

*Look for the words **vegetable scraps** in this paragraph.*

As Amy started washing, Aunt Lea brought in a bucket from outside. She told Amy to throw in the leftover vegetable scraps from their dinner plates. There were pea shells and pepper seeds, and Amy put them all in. She almost tossed in some chicken bones, but Aunt Lea stopped her. "Not those," she said.

When they finished washing the dishes, Amy carried the bucket outside. She followed Aunt Lea to a big wooden box in the garden. The box had round holes in its sides and a lid, and it was wrapped with wire mesh.

Remember what is in the bucket!

"This is the secret to my garden," Aunt Lea said. She lifted the lid and told Amy to empty the bucket inside. She took a shovel and mixed up the contents of the box. Amy watched, and she saw a huge pile of black dirt mixed with food scraps. Where the shovel turned the dirt, she saw worms and other crawly things.

"How is this the secret to your garden?" asked Amy.

"You know plants grow in the soil, right?"

"Yes, but…"

"Well, these worms and little bugs eat our vegetable scraps," explained Aunt Lea, "and they turn our garbage into fresh earth."

"How?"

"They eat the earth and…let it out after they digest it. Then the digested stuff becomes part of the earth. It is good for the soil."

"They eat it and…eewwww!"

"That's how most of the dirt you see is made. It's called compost, and this is a compost box. The worms and bugs break the scraps down with their bodies so that the soil becomes rich with nutrients for growing plants."

"Let's put it in the garden now!" Amy urged. She wanted to dig up some worms.

"Not yet. It takes months to break down the vegetables," Aunt Lea told her. "But you can help me spread it in the spring."

Amy asked about the wire and the holes in the box.

"The fencing keeps animals out," explained Aunt Lea. "They'd love to eat our leftovers! The holes are for air."

"So the worms can breathe?" asked Amy.

"Sort of," said Aunt Lea. "The compost process goes faster if oxygen can get in. That's also why I have to turn the compost with the shovel sometimes."

"Why couldn't I put in the chicken bones?"

"Some things the worms can't break down. Only vegetables can go into the compost."

When spring came, Amy helped spread the new earth. By summer, big plants grew in the garden again. One afternoon, Amy was eating fresh peas, and she didn't need Aunt Lea to remind her. Amy kept the pea shells and took them to the compost box.

"That's for next year!" she said.

Read this open-ended question about the selection. Notice that the question begins with a question word and that it asks you to find information on the page.

What happens to Aunt Lea's leftover vegetable scraps?

Aliza's Answer:

Here is Aliza's answer. Read what she wrote. Then answer the questions that follow to see what makes Aliza's answer a good one.

Aunt Lea's leftover vegetable scraps are used to make compost. First, Aunt Lea puts all the vegetable scraps into a big bucket. After that, she empties the bucket into a special box in the garden. This box is a compost box. Inside the box are worms and bugs.

The worms and bugs eat all the vegetable scraps. They digest the scraps, and their bodies break them down. Then, the digested stuff comes out of their bodies. Now it is fresh soil, which is also called compost. Last of all, Aunt Lea puts the soil back into the garden to help more vegetables grow.

What Makes Aliza's Answer Work?

Aliza's answer includes the things that test scorers look for:

✓ A clear statement of the main idea at the beginning of the answer.

✓ A clear, detailed, and organized description of what happens to the vegetable scraps.

✓ A good closing sentence.

Now take a closer look at Aliza's answer to see what makes it work.

1. Aliza begins her answer by stating the main idea. Notice that she uses part of the question in her answer.

   What is Aliza's main idea? Write her main-idea sentence here.

   _____

   _____

   _____

2. Aliza gives the steps for turning vegetable scraps into compost in order.

a. **What is the first step? Write Aliza's sentence here.**

   _____

   _____

   _____

b. **What is the second step? Write Aliza's sentence here.**

   _____

   _____

   _____

3. Aliza includes enough details to make her answer very clear and complete. One detail, in paragraph 2, is that the worms and bugs eat all the vegetable scraps.

What is another detail in paragraph 2? Write Aliza's sentence here.

_____

_____

_____

_____

4. Aliza's last sentence is a good closing for her answer. It lets her readers know that the answer is complete.

How does Aliza close her answer? Write Aliza's closing sentence here.

_____

_____

_____

_____

_____

Tools & Tips

When you describe a process, you need to be very clear. Your description will be clearer if you use words to show the order of the steps. These words are called **transition** words.

Aliza used transition words when she wrote these sentences:

✓ **First,** Aunt Lea puts all the vegetable scraps into a big bucket.

✓ **After that,** she empties the bucket into a special box in the garden.

Here are some more transition words. Add some words of your own.

Words that show what comes first:

First of all

To start

To begin

_____

_____

Words that show what comes last:

Last

Finally

At the end

_____

_____

Words that show what comes next:

Next

Then

Later

_____

_____

Words that show what comes before:

Before

Back then

Yesterday

_____

_____

Lesson 11

Strategy: Transition Words

Aliza's answer was a good one because she **organized** her description. She told what happened to the vegetable scraps in order, beginning with the first step.

When you tell how something is done or how something happened, it's important to put the steps in the right order, or *sequence*. Here are some strategies to help you:

✓ Make sure you know the correct order. Look for clues in the text. Words like **first**, **next**, and **last** will show you the order of the steps.

✓ Make sure you write the steps in the correct order. Check your answer against the information in the reading selection.

✓ Use transition words to tell the order—what's first, what's next, and what's last.

Try it with this paragraph.

> To make an egg sandwich, begin by hard-boiling the egg. The next step is to slice the egg. Slice the egg carefully so that you don't mush the egg. Last of all, put the egg slices between two pieces of bread.

1. What is the first step in making an egg sandwich? What is the clue word?

   Write the clue word here. _____

   Now write the first step in your own words. Remember to begin with a transition word or words.

   _____

   _____

2. What is the next step in making an egg sandwich? What is the clue word?

   Write the clue word here. _____

   Now write the next step in your own words. Remember to begin with a transition word or words.

   _____

   _____

3. What is the last step in making an egg sandwich? What is the clue word?

   Write the clue here. _____

   Now write the last step in your own words. Remember to begin with a transition word or words.

   _____

   _____

4. Now put it all together. How do you make an egg sandwich?

   Describe the process.

   _____
   _____
   _____
   _____
   _____
   _____
   _____
   _____
   _____
   _____
   _____
   _____
   _____
   _____
   _____
   _____

Revising and Improving a Weak Answer

In this lesson, you are going to use what you've learned to improve an answer that is not a good one. Read the selection *The Secret to the Garden* on pages 62 and 63. Then read this question about it.

> **How does the compost box help turn vegetable scraps into dirt for the garden?**

Jerome's Answer:

Here is the way Jerome answered this question.

The box holds the vegetable scraps. Animals can't get at them. The scraps get eaten by worms.

Improving Jerome's Answer

Jerome has answered the question in a very general way.

✓ He explains that the scraps go inside the compost box.

✓ He has given two details about what happens after the scraps are put into the compost box.

✓ He needs to give more details to explain how the compost box works.

Imagine that you wrote Jerome's answer. Ask yourself the following questions to help you revise and improve it.

1. Have I stated the main idea of my answer? What can I add to make the main idea clear?

   Write an opening sentence here.

   _____

   _____

   _____

   _____

2. Have I said how the box keeps animals from getting into the vegetable scraps? What details can I add to this part of my answer?
Rewrite your sentence here, adding these details.

_____

_____

_____

_____

3. Have I given enough details to explain what happens in the box when the worms eat the scraps? What details can I add to this part of my answer?
Write a new sentence here, adding these details.

_____

_____

_____

_____

4. Have I said how the box helps break down the vegetable scraps? What details can I add to this part of my answer?
Write a new sentence here, adding these details.

_____

_____

_____

_____

SCORE BUILDER

Sometimes it's hard to tell if you need more details. Here are some ways to help you decide if you need to add more.

Check the length of your answer.

✓ Have you written only one or two sentences?

✓ Have you filled only a small part of the space provided for an answer?

✓ If you answered YES to either of these questions, you probably haven't included enough details. Add more!

Pretend you have never read the selection.

✓ Does your answer make sense?

✓ Do you have questions about things that aren't clear, or do you want more information?

✓ If you answered YES to any of these questions, you probably haven't included enough details. Add more!

Check the reading selection.

✓ Does the selection have many more details than you included in your answer?

✓ Does the selection have a whole paragraph about something that you've described in only a few words?

✓ If you answered YES to either of these questions, you probably haven't included enough details. Add more!

Use this guide to help you decide whether you need more details when you write your answer to the question on page 73.

Responding on Your Own

Here is one more question about the selection, *The Secret to the Garden*. This time, answer it on your own. Plan your answer carefully. Think about what you have learned from studying Aliza's good answer and improving Jerome's weak answer. You should also use the following to help you write your answer:

✓ the **strategy** you have practiced (transition words)

✓ the tips you were given in **Tools & Tips**

✓ the reminders in the **Score Builder**

Read this question.

> **How did Amy help her Aunt Lea with the compost? Support your answer with details from the reading selection.**

Write your answer on the lines below.

_____

_____

_____

_____

_____

_____

_____

_____

_____

_____

_____

_____

_____

_____

HINT!

Remember that the test scorers look for the following things:

* A clear statement of the main idea at the beginning of the answer.

* A well-organized answer, with the steps in order.

* Enough details to make the answer complete.

* A good closing sentence.

Reader's Response!
Revise & Edit

When you have finished writing, exchange papers with a partner. As you read each other's work, answer the questions below.

1 Do you think the writer's main idea is stated clearly?   ___Yes ___ No
If you do, explain why. If you don't, explain why not.
Write your response here.

_____

_____

2 Did the writer include enough supporting details?   ___ Yes ___ No
If not, what needs to be added?
Write your response here.

_____

_____

3 Are the details in an order that makes sense?   ___ Yes ___ No
If not, what needs to be changed?
Write your response here.

_____

_____

4 Is there a closing sentence?   ___ Yes ___ No

5 Has the writer followed all the SLAMS rules?   ___ Yes ___ No
If not, which rules were not followed?
Check all the rules that apply.

S ___   L ___   A ___   M ___   S ___

6 **Give the paper back to your partner to revise and edit.**

Reviewing the Question

Here are some ways that a test might ask a question about what is on the page. Pay special attention to the words in **dark type**.

- **How** do worms make fresh earth?
- **Where** does Aunt Lea put her vegetable scraps?
- **What** happens to the vegetables in the compost box?
- **Why** doesn't Amy's aunt put chicken bones in the compost box?
- **When** is the new earth ready to go into the garden?

The words in dark type are all **question words**. They point to information in the selection that will help answer the question.

Watch for question words in an open-ended question. A question word often means that you need to find information on the page.

Reading Between the Lines

In the last unit, you answered questions about what was "on the page." You found the answers in the reading selections.

Sometimes when you read, understanding the words is not all you have to do. You also need to figure out information that is *not* on the page. You figure out this information from hints and clues in the text. This is called **making inferences**. In other words, you are **reading <u>between</u> the lines**.

Here are some examples. See if you can figure out what's "between the lines."

- "Here I come, ready or not!" Roger called, but Tug just smiled.
- "Mosquito hawk" is another name for a dragonfly.
- Anna entered the air-conditioned room and breathed a sigh of relief.

If you read between the lines, you figured out that:

- The boys are playing hide-and-seek, and Tug thinks he is well hidden.
- Dragonflies eat mosquitoes.
- It's hot where Anna just came from.

None of this information was in the sentences, but you were able to make inferences and figure it out for yourself. *You read between the lines.*

Lesson 14

What Makes a Good Answer?

Read the story below. The open-ended questions that follow ask you to read "between the lines." You will make inferences to explain what happens in the story and why it happens.

The Mystery Fish of Hawaii

The state of Hawaii is made up of many islands. On many of the islands, huge cliffs rise near the edge of the sea. Streams rush over the cliffs, making a waterfall. One of Hawaii's most famous waterfalls is Hi'ilawe (say *hee-ee-LAH-way*).

If you go to the top of Hi'ilawe, you will see something very strange. Small fish called gobies swim in the stream that feeds the waterfall. A goby is not much bigger than your little finger. How did the gobies get there? The answer is hard to believe.

Why do you think the suckers are important?

When a baby goby is born, it is swept away by the waterfall. The goby drops more than a thousand feet. Then the stream carries it into the sea. The baby goby doesn't grow up in the ocean. It finds a shallow pool in the rocks of the nearby shore. Here, two of the goby's fins grow together under its chest. The fins form a sucker, or a suction cup, like the suckers on the arms of an octopus.

Then, when the goby is almost an inch long and weighs very little, it swims back into the ocean, and it begins to climb to the top of the sea cliff! It uses its sucker to hold on to the rock wall behind the waterfall. When it lets go, it beats its tail madly to slide upward. The goby repeats this action more than 12,000 times. It won't give up until it reaches the top.

The goby finishes growing in the small pools along the side of the stream. There's lots of good food here and no enemies. The goby spends most of the rest of its life taking it easy.

Read this question.

> **The baby goby grows up in rock pools at the edge of the ocean. What do you think keeps the baby goby from being swept out to sea by big waves? Use details from the story to explain your answer.**

Ken's Answer:

Here is Ken's answer. Read what he wrote. Then answer the questions that follow to learn why Ken's answer is a good one.

> I think that the goby's suckers keep it from being swept out to sea by big waves.
>
> Two of the goby's fins under its body grow together. They make a sucker like the ones an octopus has. A sucker holds onto things. The goby's sucker could hold onto the rocks. That way, the goby would be safe inside the rock pools. The waves couldn't wash it away.

What Makes Ken's Answer Work?

Ken does all the things that the test scorers look for:
- ✓ He states his main idea clearly.
- ✓ He answers all the parts of the question.
- ✓ He uses a lot of details from the story to explain his answer.
- ✓ He writes clear and complete sentences.

Let's take a closer look at Ken's answer to see why it is a good one.

1. Ken begins with a sentence that answers the question. The sentence also uses part of the question.

   In which sentence does Ken do this? Write Ken's sentence here.

   _____

   _____

   _____

2. Ken uses details from the story to explain where the goby's suckers come from.

   In which sentences does Ken do this? Write Ken's sentences here.

   _____

   _____

   _____

3. Ken also uses details from the story to show how the goby's suckers keep it safe from the waves.

   In which sentences does Ken do this? Write Ken's sentences here.

   _____

   _____

   _____

   _____

4. Ken writes clear, complete sentences that begin with a capital letter and end with a period.

   Find a sentence that you think is clear and complete. Write Ken's sentence here.

   _____

   _____

   _____

Tools & Tips

Before you read a selection, you can learn many things about it. You can look for clues in the title and in the illustrations, and you can find clues in the text by skimming.

Take another look at *The Mystery Fish of Hawaii*.

1. What does the title tell you?

_____

_____

2. What do you learn from the picture?

_____

_____

3. Skim the text. Find part of a sentence that looks different. What does this tell you?

_____

_____

When you take a good look at the selection before you read, you prepare for reading.

✓ The title prepares you for what the story will be about.

✓ The illustrations prepare you for details you will find.

✓ Text that is printed differently than the rest might mean that this information is special.

Lesson 15

Strategy: Write an Umbrella Statement

Good writers use special strategies that help them answer questions. This is your chance to learn and practice one of the strategies that good readers and writers use. We call it "Writing an Umbrella Statement."

Ken's Answer:

Let's look at the first sentence of Ken's answer:

> I think that the goby's suckers keep it from being swept out to sea by big waves.

Notice two things about Ken's sentence:

✓ Ken's sentence answers the question in few words. The rest of the complete answer gives details and support from the selection.

✓ Ken's sentence repeats part of the question. This helps the reader know what question is being answered.

Ken's sentence is an **umbrella statement**. It covers both the question and its answer, the way an umbrella covers you from the rain.

1. Suppose a question asks, "What is unusual about Hi'ilawe Falls?" Which answer makes the best umbrella statement?

   a. It's a thousand feet tall.

   b. Hi'ilawe Falls is unusual because it's a thousand feet tall.

2. Suppose a question asks, "What will you find in the stream at the top of the waterfall?" Which answer makes the best umbrella statement?

   a. You'll find small fish called gobies in the stream at the top of the waterfall.

   b. There are gobies there.

3. Suppose a question asks, "Where do baby gobies grow up?" Which answer makes the best umbrella statement?

a. in rock pools

b. The baby gobies grow up in rock pools near the shore.

4. Suppose a question asks, "Why don't you find other kinds of fish in the stream above the waterfall?" Which answer makes the best umbrella statement?

a. You don't find other fish in the stream above the waterfall because they don't have suckers. So they can't climb the waterfall.

b. because they can't get up there and they don't have suckers.

5. Try writing your own umbrella statement. Suppose a question asks, "What do you think happens to many baby gobies before they grow a sucker?" **Write your answer on the lines below.**

_____

_____

_____

_____

_____

_____

Lesson 16

Revising and Improving a Weak Answer

The next step in learning to write a good answer is to try improving an answer that is not successful. Read *The Mystery Fish of Hawaii* again. Then read and answer the question below about it.

> **How do you think the goby's small size helps it when it climbs Hi'ilawe Falls?**

Della's Answer:

Look at the answer Della wrote.

> It's not very big. It climbs behind the falls because it has a sucker.

Improving Della's Answer

Della has answered the question in a very general way.

✓ She says that the goby isn't very big.

✓ She says that the goby uses its sucker to climb the falls.

But Della's answer is very short. It's not clear what she's writing about. Also Della hasn't really answered the question. She has explained that the goby's sucker lets it climb behind the falls, but she hasn't explained how the goby's small size helps it climb the falls. That was the question she should have answered.

Della hasn't read between the lines. She hasn't provided enough details from the story in her answer. The test scorers would not give her answer a good score.

Answer the following questions to help you revise and improve Della's answer.

1. Read the first sentence of Della's answer. Is it clear what Della is talking about? If not, rewrite the sentence.
   Write the new sentence here.

   _____

   _____

   _____

2. Has Della mentioned how the goby's size helps it climb behind the waterfall? If not, write about it.

Write the sentence here.

_____

_____

_____

3. Has Della thought about how a goby's size would affect its climbing ability? Which would climb with less effort—a heavy fish or a light fish?

Write your answer here.

_____

_____

_____

4. **Now rewrite the answer below. Use the new sentences you wrote. Include as many details from the story as you can, if they help answer the question.**

_____

_____

_____

_____

_____

_____

_____

_____

_____

_____

SCORE BUILDER

Good writers vary their sentences. They don't write short, choppy sentences. The sentences below are examples of choppy sentences.

The baby goby grows a sucker. It swims up the stream. It swims to the waterfall.

You won't score your best if you write short, choppy sentences. Here are four better ways to write these same sentences:

✓ The baby goby grows a sucker, swims upstream, and climbs the falls.

✓ The baby goby grows a sucker. Then it swims upstream and climbs the falls.

✓ After the baby goby grows a sucker, it swims upstream and climbs the falls.

✓ When the baby goby has grown a sucker, it swims upstream to climb the falls.

Try it! Rewrite each group of sentences below.

1 Hawaii has many cliffs. They rise from the sea. They are tall.

Write your new sentence or sentences here.

_____

_____

2. A stream feeds the waterfall. It has small fish. They swim in the stream.

Write your new sentence or sentences here.

_____

_____

Responding on Your Own

Now you are going to answer another question about the story, *The Mystery Fish of Hawaii*. This time you will answer without models or questions to help you.

As you plan and write your answer, think about what you have learned from studying Ken's answer and improving Della's answer. You should also use the following to help you write your answer:

✓ the **strategy** you have practiced (writing an umbrella statement)

✓ the tips in **Tools & Tips**

✓ the reminders in the **Score Builder**

Notice that this question, like the first two, asks you to read between the lines and explain something that might not be stated directly in the story.

Read this question.

> **The native people of Hawaii have a saying: "Kulia I ka nu'u." It means, "Go for the mountain top." An Olympic athlete might say that the proverb means "Go for the gold." A coach might say, "Be the best you can be." Explain how the story *The Mystery Fish of Hawaii* teaches the lesson "Kulia I ka nu'u."**

Write your answer on the lines below.

_____

_____

_____

_____

_____

_____

_____

_____

_____

_____

_____

HINT!

Remember that the test scorers will be looking for the following things:

* A clear and complete sentence that tells the main idea.

* A complete answer to the question.

* Supporting details from the story.

* Clears and complete sentences.

Reader's Response!
Revise & Edit

When you have finished writing, exchange papers with a partner. As you read each other's work, answer the questions below.

1   Did the writer answer the question?   ___Yes ___ No

2   Did the writer repeat the question in the answer?   ___Yes ___ No

3   Did the writer give clear reasons for the explanation?   ___Yes ___ No
If not, what needs to be added or changed?
Write your response here.

_____

_____

_____

_____

_____

4   Has the writer followed all the SLAMS rules?   ___ Yes ___ No
If not, which rules were not followed?
Check all the rules that apply.

S ___   L ___   A ___   M ___   S ___

5   **Give the paper back to your partner to revise and edit.**

Reviewing the Question

A question about reading between the lines can be asked in many ways. Here are a few you might find.

Questions about *why* or *how* something happens. For example:

- **Why** isn't a goby hurt when it falls down the waterfall?

- **How** fast could a T. rex run?

- **What made** Lucia think about designing a new can opener?

Questions about how a character in a story feels or why he or she does something. For example:

- **Why** did Jeannie refuse to play shortstop?

- **What kind** of person is Roger?

- **What made** Fran turn against Ellie?

Continued on page 90

Reviewing the Question

Continued from page 89

Questions that ask you to compare two things, or to guess what will happen next. For example:

- **Who do you think** will win the contest?

- **Who is really** the better sport—Sandy or Gil?

- **What can Leah do** when Mrs. Griswold finds out what really happened in the haunted house?

You can't always tell an inference question just by looking at it. If you don't find the answer in the story, then you probably need to read between the lines.

Reading Beyond the Lines

In Unit 4, you learned how to read what is on the page. In Unit 5, you learned how to read between the lines. Now you are ready to learn about reading **beyond** the lines. Below are some examples of questions that ask you to read beyond the lines. See if you can find the phrase that asks you to "read beyond the lines."

- How would you feel about giving up TV for a week? Use details from the selection and from your own experience to explain your answer.

- How would you persuade someone to give up junk food? Use information from the selection and from your own experience for support.

- Which twin would you want to be like? Use details from the selection and from you own experience in your answer.

What information do these questions have in common? That's right. You have to go **beyond the lines** and add your own opinion. You still have to use details from the story. Those details help support what you write.

Lesson 18

What Makes a Good Answer?

Read this selection, then read the question on page 94.

Stamp Collecting

Carlita didn't have much time. Big Gramps's seventy-fifth birthday was in two weeks. She wanted to get him a present that he would keep forever.

How does Carlita feel about Big Gramps?

Carlita always loved the stories Big Gramps told about growing up on a farm in Georgia. He used to say that he was poor but didn't know it. There was always something to eat and stories to hear on the farm. "My momma—your great grandma—wanted us to grow up knowing things. She was a teacher at the school for African-American children."

When he got to that part, Big Gramps always stopped. "Did you know that once upon a time, African-American children and white children couldn't go to school together?" he would ask.

They all nodded and waited for the next question.

"Do you know who made things change?" he asked next. Then they would all shout out the names of people they knew who had fought for change—Rosa Parks, Dr. Martin Luther King, Jr., even Jackie Robinson.

"That's right," Big Gramps nodded. "They made things change. So did my momma and daddy and everybody else who marched for freedom."

One time Carlita asked, "Did you ever march, Big Gramps?"

He gave a big smile. "Yes, I did."

"Were you scared?" cousin Bernice asked.

"Did you go to jail like Dr. King?" asked another cousin.

"No, I didn't, but other people did. And soon all kinds of people from all over the country came down here and marched."

The next day, Carlita's class took a field trip into town. First, they went to the firehouse and the library. Then they ate lunch in the park. Their next stop was the post office.

Two by two they went inside. Ms. Turner, their teacher, said, "Look around. What history do you see?"

Carlita looked at the floor. Nothing there. Then she looked up. On the far wall hung a huge poster filled with paintings of African Americans. Carlita recognized Dr. King right away, and Jackie Robinson, too. Their pictures were also in her classroom. She saw pictures of other people she didn't know. If only Big Gramps could see.

That's it! Carlita thought. That's the present for Big Gramps.

Carlita realized Ms. Turner was telling them something. "The post office wants you each to have a booklet. The booklet shows all the stamps that have been created to honor African-Americans. What do you say?"

"Thank you," everyone answered.

Carlita thought, "Now Big Gramps can tell us stories forever, and he has pictures to go with them."

What connection can you make to Carlita's field trip?

What present might you give someone in your family?

Read this question.

> **Think about a friend or relative you know who you admire. Who is this person and why do you admire him or her? Use details from the selection and from your own experience to write your answer.**

Julio's Answer.

Read what Julio wrote. Then answer the questions that follow to see why Julio's answer is a good one.

In my family, our grandma is the person with the best stories. Abuelita Inez tells us about the old days, just like the grandpa in the story.

When she was little, her family moved to America. Every day she walked to school and back again. When she got home, she told her parents in English what she learned. She never missed a day of school because her parents wanted to learn, too.

Once I told her I was too tired for school. That's when she told me her story. Now I only miss school when I'm very sick.

What Makes Julio's Answer Work?

Julio's answer includes the things the test scorers look for.

✓ A clear statement of the main idea at the beginning.

✓ A reference to a detail in the story. This shows that Julio has made a connection to the story.

✓ An example from Julio's own life to show what his grandmother does for the family.

✓ A good closing sentence.

Now take a closer look at Julio's answer.

1. Julio begins his answer by stating the main idea.

   What is Julio's main idea? Write his main-idea sentence here.

   _____

   _____

   _____

2. Julio makes a reference to the selection he read.

   Write Julio's sentence here.

   _____

   _____

   _____

3. Julio includes enough details to make his answer very clear and easy to understand. One detail, in paragraph 2, is that Abuelita Inez and her family moved to American when she was little.

   What is another detail in paragraph 2? Write Julio's detail sentence here.

   _____

   _____

   _____

4. Julio's grandmother ends her story with a sentence that tells what she learned from her experience.

   What does Abuelita Inez learn from her experience? Write the sentence that tells what Abuelita Inez learned.

   _____

   _____

   _____

5. Julio's last sentence is a good closing sentence for his answer. It tells the reader what Julio learned from his grandmother's stories.

   How does Julio close his answer? Write Julio's closing sentence here.

   _____

   _____

   _____

Tools & Tips

When you describe something that happened to you, you need to use lots of details. Where do the details come from? They come from your memory. Your memory is one of your most important tools!

Don't worry if you don't remember things exactly. Your memory helps you remember lots of things. For example, your memory helps you describe a scene from your favorite movie. You don't have to think too hard about your favorite movie because you've probably seen the movie more than once. It has been "recorded" in your mind.

This kind of memory is "built-in." When you close your eyes and think about your favorite part of the movie, you see the characters, where they are, how they look, what they are doing, and what you hear. You probably can explain to someone why you like it so much, too. Let's call this memory your "Eye Memory."

When you want to write about a story from your own experience, close your eyes and pretend that you are seeing it like a scene in your favorite movie. Work with an adult—either in your classroom or at home—so you will have a record of your scene. Then close your eyes and see the scene as it happened. When you finish, rewind the scene and see it again. This time tell the adult what you see, and ask the adult to write it down. When you finish, you will have a long paragraph—maybe even two. You can use this scene whenever you need it.

Lesson 19

Strategy: Making Connections

Reading beyond the lines often asks you to **make a connection** between the story and an experience of your own. You might not know ahead of time what the story will be about. There is, however, a way to prepare for this kind of question.

Most reading selections in tests are chosen because they tell about something that everyone knows. The story may take place in a country far away from America, and the everyday life of the people may be very different. Even so, many things will be familiar to you because people throughout the world share common needs and emotions. They laugh. They play. They worry. They have friends.

Here are some story themes that most people experience.

- ✓ Starting a new school
- ✓ Making a friend
- ✓ Worrying about tests
- ✓ Learning from other people
- ✓ Playing a new game
- ✓ Enjoying a birthday party
- ✓ Taking a trip to a new place
- ✓ Feeling sad when a friend moves
- ✓ Going some place special with your family

Add other ideas that you think people experience. The ideas can be ones you've experienced, or experiences you have heard or learned about.

_____

_____

_____

_____

_____

_____

_____

Read the story descriptions below. Pick one that you connect to. Use your "eye memory" to remember your experience. Tell a partner about your idea.

1. Story Idea: Abe and Esther are moving to America. They have never traveled by plane before. The trip is long, but someone tells them stories to make the time pass quickly.

    Make a connection to this story. Maybe you have taken a trip or met someone new while traveling. Write some ideas. Then tell a partner about your connection.

    _____

    _____

    _____

2. Story Idea: Travis likes to play soccer. His best friend, Jed, doesn't. Travis and Jed have been friends since kindergarten. They don't see each other much anymore. They decide to find something they can do together.

    Make a connection to this story. Who have you known for a long time? How are you the same and different? Write some ideas. Then tell a partner about your connection.

    _____

    _____

    _____

3. Story Idea: Jeng Li is happy about his birthday party. Everyone he likes has come to his outdoor party. The weather is perfect, too. Jeng Li even smashes the piñata open.

    Make a connection. Think about a party, picnic, or special event you went to. What was it like? Write some ideas. Then tell a partner about your connection.

    _____

    _____

    _____

Lesson 20

Revising and Improving a Weak Answer

The next step in learning to write a good answer is to try to improve an answer that is not a good one. Look again at the story, *Stamp Collecting*. Read this question.

> **Did you ever go on a field trip that you really enjoyed or that you learned a lot from? What made it fun, or what did you learn? Use details from the selection and from your own experience in your answer.**

Josh's Answer:

Read Josh's answer below. Then use the questions that follow to help you revise and improve his answer.

> We went to a firehouse. The firefighters were nice. I learned a lot.

Improving Josh's Answer

Josh has answered the question in a very general way.

✓ He tells about part of the field trip.

✓ He says that the firefighters were nice.

✓ He says he learned a lot.

Josh's answer has some problems.

✓ It is very short.

✓ It doesn't tell many details about Josh's trip.

✓ It doesn't tell any details from the story *Stamp Collecting*.

✓ It doesn't say what Josh has learned.

For these reasons, the test scorers would not give Josh's answer a high score.

Imagine you are Josh. Think about what you might see and learn on a field trip to a firehouse.

Answer the following questions to help revise and improve Josh's answer.

1. Josh says that the firefighters were nice.

What do you imagine the firefighters said or did that made Josh think they were nice? Tell two or three things that the firefighters did. Write your answer here.

_____

_____

_____

_____

_____

2. Josh saw and did many things in the firehouse.

What details can you imagine about the firehouse? Write the details here.

_____

_____

_____

_____

_____

3. Look at the paragraph in *Stamp Collecting* that begins, "The next day Carlita's class took a field trip…." Read this paragraph and the two paragraphs after it.

Could Josh have seen anything like Carlita saw? Tell what it was and explain how it was like what Carlita saw. Write your answer here.

_____

_____

_____

_____

_____

_____

4. Josh probably learned many things on his trip to the firehouse.

   Tell one or two things that you imagine he might have learned from the trip. Write the details here.

   _____

   _____

   _____

   _____

5. Now rewrite the answer to the question.

   Did you ever go on a field trip that you really enjoyed or that you learned a lot from? What made it fun, or what did you learn? Use your answers to the questions above. Write your answer here.

   _____

   _____

   _____

   _____

   _____

   _____

   _____

   _____

   _____

   _____

   _____

   _____

   _____

   _____

   _____

SCORE BUILDER

In the "Tools & Tips" section of this chapter, you learned about using your **eye memory** to help you remember details. You closed your eyes and pretended to see details of an experience, just as if you were watching a movie.

Just for fun, try out your eye memory of the last class field trip you took, or another event your class enjoyed.

1 What place did you go to on your last field trip, or what did your class do?

Write your answer here.

_____

_____

_____

Now use your Eye Memory to help you answer the following questions.

2 What do you see when you first come to this place?

Write your answer here.

_____

_____

_____

Continued on page 104

SCORE BUILDER

Continued from page 103

3 What is the most interesting thing you see?
Write your answer here.

_____

_____

_____

4 Do you hear any interesting sounds? What are they?
Write your answer here.

_____

_____

_____

5 What is the first thing you did?
Write your answer here.

_____

_____

_____

6 What was your favorite part?
Write your answer here.

_____

_____

_____

Responding on Your Own

Here is another question about the story, *Stamp Collecting*. This time, you are going to write your own answer, without models or questions to help you. As you plan and write your answer, think about what you have learned from studying Julio's answer and improving Josh's answer. You should also use the following to help you write your answer:

✓ the **strategy** you have practiced (making connections)

✓ the tips in **Tools & Tips**

✓ the reminders in the **Score Builder**

This question asks you to read beyond the lines. You will tell about something that happened to you. You will connect your experience to the story you have read.

> **Think about a time when you wanted to find the perfect present for someone in your family or a very close friend. How did you decide what to buy? Why was the present special? Use details from the selection and from your own experience. Write your answer on the lines below.**

HINT!

Remember that the test scorers will look for the following things:

* A clear statement of the main idea at the beginning of the answer.

* A reference to something in the story to show that you have made a connection.

* An example from your own life.

* A good closing sentence.

Reader's Response!
Revise & Edit

When you have finished writing about *Stamp Collecting*, exchange papers with a partner. As you read each other's work, answer the questions below.

1 Did the writer answer the question? ___Yes ___ No

2 Did the writer make a clear statement of the main idea at the beginning? ___Yes ___ No

3 Did the writer make a connection to the story? Explain why or why not. ___ Yes ___ No

Write your response here.

_____

_____

_____

4 Did the writer use enough details to tell about his or her experience? ___Yes ___ No
If not, what needs to be added or changed?

Write your response here.

_____

_____

_____

5 Has the writer followed all the SLAMS rules? ___ Yes ___ No
If not, which rules were not followed?

Check all the rules that apply.

S ___   L ___   A ___   M ___   S ___

6 **Give the paper back to your partner to revise and edit.**

Reviewing the Question

It's easy to identify a question that asks you to read beyond the lines. These questions have two parts.

Part 1. This part asks a question about something you saw, felt, experienced, or remember. For example:

- Did you ever have to do something you really didn't like?

- How do you like to spend your free time?

- Who do you think is a hero?

- What was the hardest thing you ever had to do?

Part 2. This part asks you to connect your answer to the story you just read. For example:

- Use details from the selection and from your own experience to explain your answer.

When you see questions that have these two parts, remember that you need to read beyond the lines. Use the details or the main idea of the selection to decide what story from your own experience you will tell. The connection can be based on something that happened to you or to someone you know.

Read the selection and answer the questions that follow.

Zack Finds His Dog

All Zack wanted for his birthday was a dog. When his birthday was just two weeks away, Zack told his mother, "I'd really, really like a dog."

Zack's mother explained that a dog was a lot of responsibility. "If you agree to take good care of it," she said, "you can have one."

"So, how do we find a dog?" asked Zack. "Do we go to the pet store?"

"Instead of buying a dog," his mother said, "I think we should adopt one from a shelter. So many homeless dogs live in animal shelters. They need good homes."

The next day, Zack and his mom visited the animal shelter in their town. Dogs of all sizes sat in their cages, looking eager and excited. Some dogs were old, and some were young. Many barked. Some just looked at Zack with their big brown eyes.

While Zack checked out the dogs, a man who worked at the animal shelter asked his mother a lot of questions. She had to fill out a form with even more questions about their apartment and their family. The man said he would also have to visit their home before they were allowed to adopt a dog.

"Why?" asked Zack.

"To make sure we have a good place for a dog to live," explained his mother.

"I found the dog I want!" Zack said suddenly. He was grinning at a small, spotted dog with big eyes. The dog seemed to grin back at him. Its tongue stuck out the side of its mouth. It wagged its curly tail when it heard Zack's voice. The man said the dog was a male and had no name.

"I'll name him Bugsy," said Zack.

"Why 'Bugsy'?" asked his mother.

"Because his eyes are bugging out of his head!" Zack laughed. The dog wagged his tail.

"He likes you," said the man from the animal shelter.

Later that week, the man came to visit. He walked around the apartment with Zack and his mother. He explained that Bugsy would need a place to eat, room to play, and somewhere warm to sleep. He made Zack and his mom promise to take care of Bugsy if he got sick.

"Bugsy will need a walk twice every day," the man told them.

"That will be Zack's job," Zack's mother replied.

The man told Zack that he would let them know if they were approved to adopt Bugsy. Zack was nervous. Why did they have to wait? What if they weren't approved? His mother told him that the man had to make sure they were a good family for Bugsy.

"Of course we are!" said Zack. "I mean, I love Bugsy already."

"Be patient," his mother told him. "Soon we'll know."

In a few days, they did. The man from the animal shelter called to say Bugsy was theirs.

On Zack's birthday, Zack and his mother went to the shelter. Zack's mother paid for Bugsy's shots and signed some papers. Then Zack picked up his new pet and carried him out.

"This is my best birthday ever!" said Zack.

Bugsy agreed. He couldn't stop wagging his tail.

1 Reading What Is on the Page

What did Zack and his mother have to do before they could adopt Bugsy? Use details from the reading selection to support your answer.

_____

_____

_____

_____

_____

_____

_____

_____

_____

_____

_____

_____

_____

_____

_____

_____

_____

_____

_____

2 Reading Between the Lines

Why did the animal shelter make Zack and his mother wait before they could adopt Bugsy?
Use your own ideas and details from the selection in your answer.

_____

_____

_____

_____

_____

_____

_____

_____

_____

_____

_____

_____

_____

_____

_____

_____

_____

3 Reading Beyond the Lines

How would you take care of a pet? Where would you keep it? How would you keep it clean? What else would you do for your pet? Use your own ideas and details from the selection to support your answer.

_____

_____

_____

_____

_____

_____

_____

_____

_____

_____

_____

_____

_____

_____

_____

_____

_____

_____